SKILLET
AWAKE

AUTHENTIC **GUITAR TAB EDITION**

www.skillet.com
www.myspace.com/skilletmusic
www.atlanticrecords.com

Alfred

Produced by
Alfred Music Publishing Co., Inc.
P.O. Box 10003
Van Nuys, CA 91410-0003
alfred.com

Printed in USA.

ISBN-10: 0-7390-6604-8
ISBN-13: 978-0-7390-6604-1

Management: Zachary Kelm for Q Management Group, LLC
Album Art Direction & Design: Mark Obriski
Art Manager: Kristie Borgmann

Photography: David Molnar

CONTENTS

HERO

I'm just a step away

I'm just a breath away

Losing my faith today

(Falling off the edge today)

I am just a man

Not superhuman

(I'm not superhuman)

Someone save me from the hate

It's just another war

Just another family torn

(Falling from my faith today)

Just a step from the edge

Just another day in the world we live

I need a hero to save me now

I need a hero

(Save me now)

I need a hero to save my life

A hero'll save me

(Just in time)

I gotta fight today

To live another day

Speaking my mind today

(My voice will be heard today)

I've gotta make a stand

But I am just a man

(I'm not superhuman)

My voice will be heard today

It's just another war

Just another family torn

(My voice will be heard today)

It's just another kill

The countdown begins to destroy ourselves

Who's gonna fight for what's right

Who's gonna help us survive

We're in the fight of our lives

(And we're not ready to die)

Who's gonna fight for the weak

Who's gonna make 'em believe

I've got a hero

(I've got a hero)

Living in me

I'm gonna fight for what's right

Today I'm speaking my mind

And if it kills me tonight

(I will be ready to die)

A hero's not afraid to give his life

A hero's gonna save me just in time

MONSTER

The secret side of me

I never let you see

I keep it caged but I can't control it

So stay away from me

The beast is ugly

I feel the rage and I just can't hold it

It's scratching on the walls

In the closet, in the halls

It comes awake and I can't control it

Hiding under the bed

In my body, in my head

Why won't somebody come and

save me from this

Make it end

I feel it deep within

It's just beneath the skin

I must confess that I feel like a monster

I hate what I've become

The nightmare's just begun

I must confess that I feel like a monster

I feel like a monster

My secret side I keep

Hid under lock and key

I keep it caged but I can't control it

'Cause if I let him out

He'll tear me up, break me down

Why won't somebody come and save me from this make it end

It's hiding in the dark

Its teeth are razor sharp

There's no escape for me

It wants my soul it wants my heart

No one can hear me scream

Maybe it's just a dream

Or maybe it's inside of me

Stop this monster

DON'T WAKE ME

I went to bed I was thinking about you
Ain't the same since I'm living without you
All the memories are getting colder
All the things that I wanna do over
Went to bed I was thinking about you
I wanna talk and laugh like we used to
When I see you in my dreams at night
It's so real but it's in my mind
And now
I guess
This is as good as it gets
Don't wake me
'Cause I don't wanna leave this dream
Don't wake me
'Cause I never seem to stay asleep enough
When it's you I'm dreaming of
I don't wanna wake up
Don't wake me
We're together just you and me
Don't wake me
'Cause we're happy like we used to be
I know I've gotta let you go
But I don't want to be alone
I know I've gotta let you go
But I don't want to wake up
I went to bed I was thinking about you
And how it felt when I finally found you
It's like a movie playing over in my head
Don't wanna look 'cause I know how it ends
All the words that I said that I wouldn't say
All the promises I made that I wouldn't break
It's last call, last song, last dance
'Cause I can't get you back, can't get a second chance
And now, I guess
This is as good as it gets
These dreams of you keep on growing stronger
It ain't a lot but it's all I have
Nothing to do but keep sleeping longer
Don't wanna stop cause I want you back

AWAKE AND ALIVE

I'm at war with the world and they
Try to pull me into the dark
I struggle to find my faith
As I'm slippin' from your arms
It's getting harder to stay awake
And my strength is fading fast
You breathe into me at last
I'm awake I'm alive
Now I know what I believe inside
Now it's my time
I'll do what I want 'cause this is my life
here, right now
I'll stand my ground and never back down
I know what I believe inside
I'm awake and I'm alive
I'm at war with the world cause I
Ain't never gonna sell my soul
I've already made up my mind
No matter what I can't be bought or sold
When my faith is getting weak
And I feel like giving in
You breathe into me again
Waking up waking up
In the dark
I can feel you in my sleep
In your arms I feel you breathe into me
Forever hold this heart that I will give to you
Forever I will live for you

ONE DAY TOO LATE

Tick tock hear the clock countdown
Wish the minute hand could be rewound
So much to do and so much I need to say
Will tomorrow be too late
Feel the moment slip into the past
Like sand through an hourglass
In the madness I guess I just forget
To do all the things I said
Time passes by
Never thought I'd wind up
One step behind
Now I've made my mind up
Today I'm gonna try a little harder

Gonna make every minute last longer
Gonna learn to forgive and forget
'Cause we don't have long, gonna make the most of it
Today I'm gonna love my enemies
Reach out to somebody who needs me
Make a change, make the world a
better place
'Cause tomorrow could be one day too late
One day too late
One day too late
Tick tock hear my life pass by
I can't erase and I can't rewind
Of all the things I regret the most I do...
Wish I'd spent more time with you
Here's my chance for a new beginning
I saved the best for a better ending
And in the end I'll make it up to you, you'll see
You'll get the very best of me
Your time is running out
You're never gonna get it back
Make the most of every moment
Stop saving the best for last

IT'S NOT ME IT'S YOU

Let's get the story straight
You were a poison
You flooded through my veins
You left me broken
You tried to make me think
That the blame was all on me
With the pain you put me through
And now I know that it's not me it's you
It's not me it's you
Always has been you
All the lies and stupid things you say and do
It's you
It's not me it's you
All the lies and pain you put me through
I know that it's not me it's you
You
You
It's not me it's you, you
So here we go again
The same fight we're always in

I don't care so why pretend
Wake me when your lecture ends
You tried to make me small
Make me fall and it's all your fault
With the pain you put me through
And now I know that it's not me it's you
Let's get the story straight
You were a poison
Flooding through my veins
You're driving me insane
And now you're gone away
I'm no longer choking
From the pain you put me through
And now I know that it's not me it's you

SHOULD'VE WHEN YOU COULD'VE

I'm done wondering where you've been
All night long when you're out with your friends
All you say, that the matter's over
But now that chapter's over
I'm done trusting you it's ended
Even after I catch you red handed
You could've been my only one
But now your chance is gone
You should've when you could've
You're gonna miss my love girl
You should, it would've been so good
You should've when I would've
Now I know I've had enough
Better luck next time girl
You should, it would've been so good
I'm done chasing you all over
May as well be chasing after thunder
Play hard to get if it makes you happy
For a change now you can start chasing me
Don't cry cause I ain't your sure thing
It ain't my fault you don't know a good thing
You could've been my only one
But now your chance is gone
Don't you understand
Don't wanna be your backup plan
Now I won't be here to clean up when it hits the fan
You tried to keep me on your leash

It's time you started chasing me

I'm done acting like I won't be

Sitting here still wishing you wanted me

Don't say that I never told you

Take some advice from somebody who knows

BELIEVE

I'm still trying to figure out how to tell you I was wrong

I can't fill the emptiness inside since you've been gone

So is it you or is it me?

I know I said things that I didn't mean

But you should've known me by now

You should've known me

If you believed

When I said

I'd be better off without you

Then you never really knew me at all

If you believed

When I said

That I wouldn't be thinking about you

You thought you knew the truth but you're wrong

You're all that I need

Just tell me that you still believe

I can't undo the things that led us to this place

But I know there's something more to us than our mistakes

So is it you or is it me

I know I'm so blind when we don't agree

But you should've known me by now

You should've known me

Cuz you're all that I want

Don't you even know me at all

You're all that I need

Just tell me that you still believe

FORGIVEN

Forgive me now cause I

Have been unfaithful

Don't ask me why cause I don't know

So many times I've tried

But was unable

But this heart belongs to you alone

Now I'm in our secret place

Alone in your embrace

Where all my wrongs have been erased

You have forgiven

All the promises and lies

All the times I compromise

All the times you were denied

You have forgiven

Forgive me I'm ashamed

I've loved another

I can't explain cause I don't know

No one can take your place

And there is no other

Forever yours and yours alone

I get down on my knees

Feel your love wash over me

There will never be another

You're the only one forever

And you know I'm yours alone

SOMETIMES

Sometimes when I lie

I know you're on to me

Sometimes I don't mind

How hateful that I can be

Sometimes I don't try

To make you happy

I don't know why I do the things I do to you but...

Sometimes I don't wanna be better

Sometimes I can't be put back together

Sometimes I find it hard to believe

There's someone else who could be

Just as messed up as me

Sometimes don't deny

That everything is wrong

Sometimes rather die

Than to admit it's my fault

Sometimes when you cry

I just don't care at all

I don't know why I do the things I do to you but...

I want someone to hurt

Like the way I hurt

It's sick but it makes me feel better

Sometimes I can't hide

The demons that I face

Sometimes don't deny

I'm sometimes sinner sometimes saint

NEVER SURRENDER

Do you know what it's like when
You're scared to see yourself
Do you know what it's like when
You wish you were someone else
Who didn't need your help to get by
Do you know what it's like
To wanna surrender
I don't wanna feel like this tomorrow
I don't wanna live like this today
Make me feel better
I wanna feel better
Stay with me here now
And never surrender
Do you now what it's like when
You're not who you wanna be
Do you know what it's like to
Be your own worst enemy
Who sees the things in me I can't hide
Do you know what it's like to wanna surrender
Make me feel better
You make me feel better
You make me feel better
Put me back together

LUCY

Hey Lucy, I remember your name
I left a dozen roses on your grave today
I'm in the grass on my knees, wipe the leaves away
I just came to talk for a while
I got some things I need to say
Now that it's over
I just wanna hold her
I'd give up all the world to see that little piece of heaven looking
back at me
Now that it's over
I just wanna hold her
I've gotta live with the choices I made
And I can't live with myself today
Hey Lucy, I remembered your birthday
They said it'd bring some closure to say your name
I know I'd do it all different if I had the chance
But all I got are these roses to give
And they can't help me make amends

Here we are
Now you're in my arms
I never wanted anything so bad
Here we are
For a brand new start
Living the life that we could've had
Me and Lucy walking hand in hand
Me and Lucy never wanna end
Just another moment in your eyes
I'll see you in another life
In heaven where we never say goodbye
Here we are, now you're in my arms
Here we are for a brand new start
Got to live with the choices I've made
And I can't live with myself today
Me and Lucy walking hand in hand
Me and Lucy never wanna end
Got to live with the choices I've made
And I can't live with myself today
Hey Lucy, I remember your name

HERO

*All gtrs. in Drop D, down 1/2 step:
⑥ = D♭ ③ = G♭
⑤ = A♭ ② = B♭
④ = D♭ ① = E♭

Words and Music by
JOHN COOPER and KOREY COOPER

*Recording sounds a half step lower than written.

Verse:

*Cue-size notes 2nd time only.

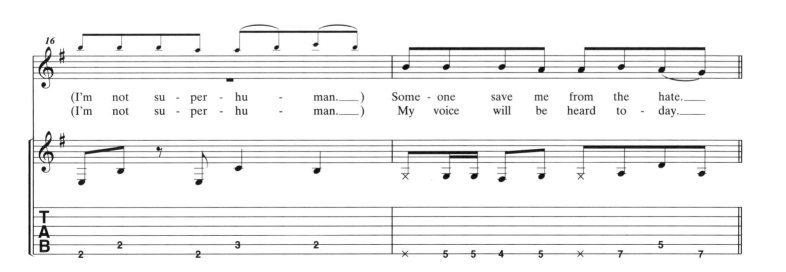

10

Chorus:

w/Rhy. **Figs. 1** *(Elec. Gtr. 1)*, **1A** *(Elec. Gtr. 2)*, **& 1B** *(Elec. Gtr. 3), each 2 times*

14

Chorus:

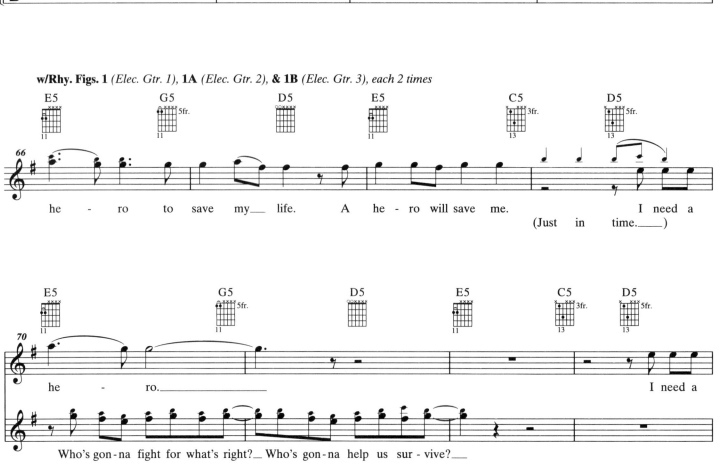

Hero - 8 - 7

MONSTER

*All gtrs. in Drop D, down 1 whole step:
⑥ = C   ③ = F
⑤ = G   ② = A
④ = C   ① = D

Words and Music by
JOHN COOPER and GAVIN BROWN

*Recording sounds a whole step lower than written.
**Elec. Gtr. 1 dbld. 2nd time.

Monster - 5 - 1

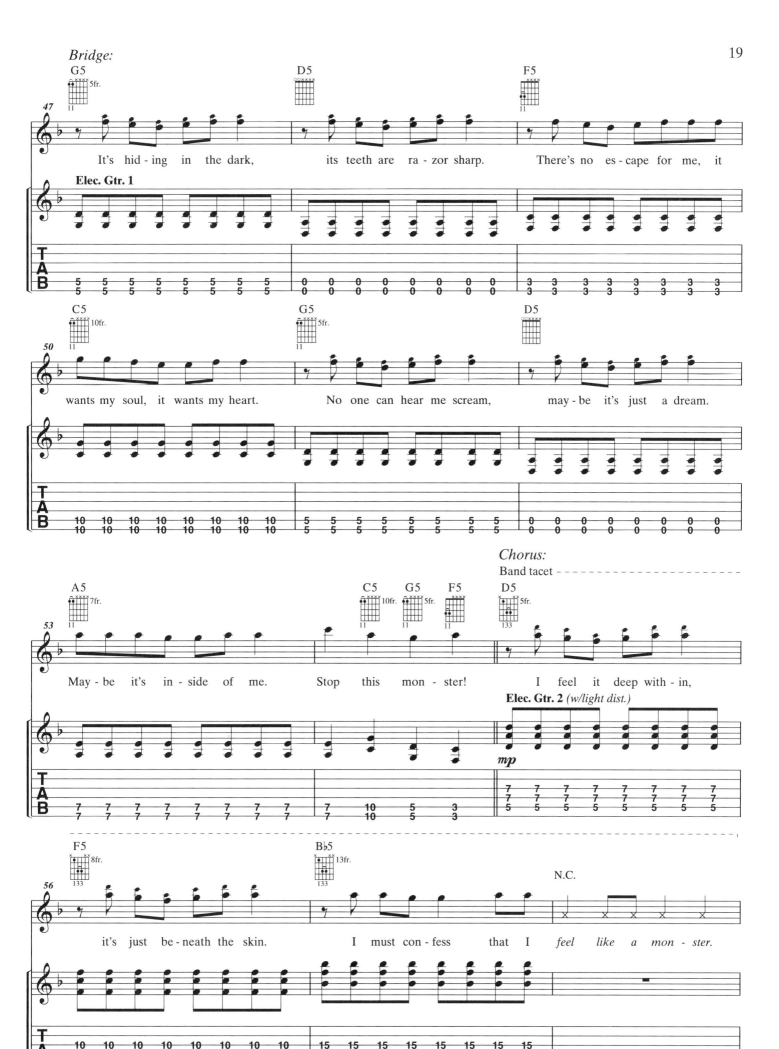

w/Rhy. Fig. 2 *(Elec. Gtr. 1) 3 times*

I hate what I've be - come, the night - mare's just be - gun. I must con - fess that I

feel like a mon - ster. I feel it deep with - in, it's just be - neath the skin.

I must con - fess that I feel like a mon - ster. I'm gon - na lose con - trol,

here's some - thing rad - i - cal. I must con - fess that I feel like a mon - ster.

I, I feel like a mon - ster. I, I feel like a mon - ster.

Elec. Gtr. 1

I, I feel like a mon - ster. I, I feel like a mon - ster.

DON'T WAKE ME

*All gtrs. tuned down 1 whole step:
⑥ = D   ③ = F
⑤ = G   ② = A
④ = C   ① = D

Words and Music by
JOHN COOPER and BRIAN HOWES

*Recording sounds a whole step lower than written.

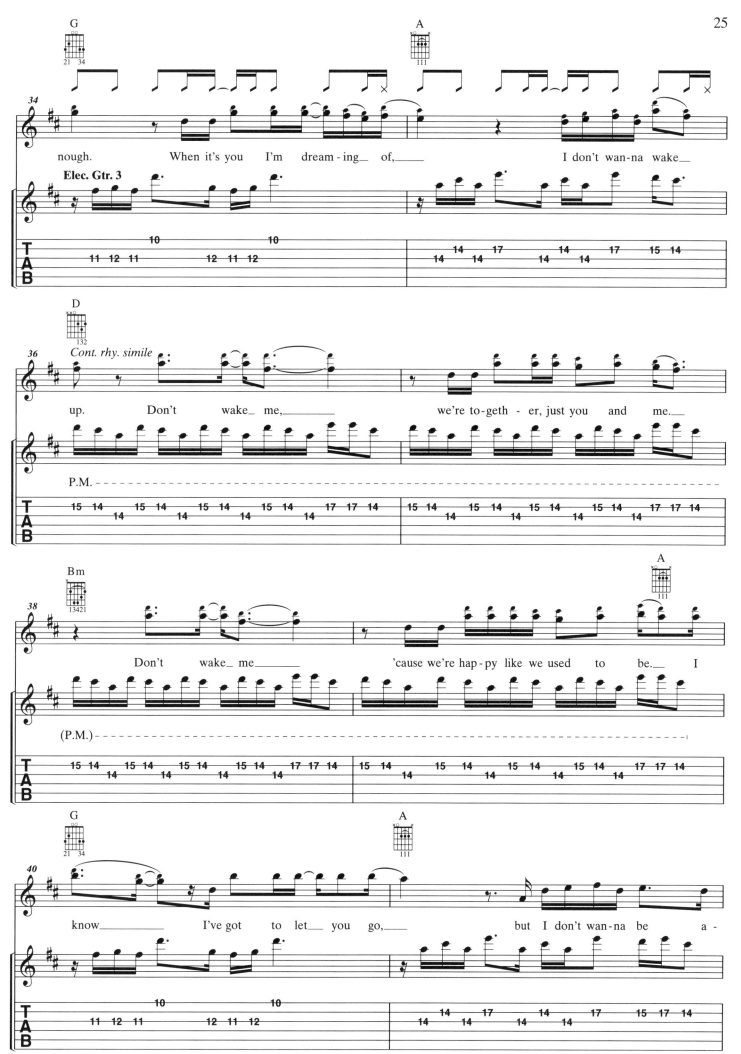

AWAKE AND ALIVE

All gtrs. in Drop D: ⑥ = D

Moderately ♩ = 84

Intro:

Words and Music by
JOHN COOPER and BRIAN HOWES

Band enters
Elec. Gtrs. 1 & 2 tacet

Band tacet - - - - - - -

Awake and Alive - 7 - 1

Chorus:

ONE DAY TOO LATE

Moderately slow ♩ = 76

Words and Music by
JOHN COOPER and BRIAN HOWES

40

IT'S NOT ME IT'S YOU

All gtrs. in Drop D: ⑥ = D

Words and Music by
JOHN COOPER

Moderately slow ♩ = 86

Intro:

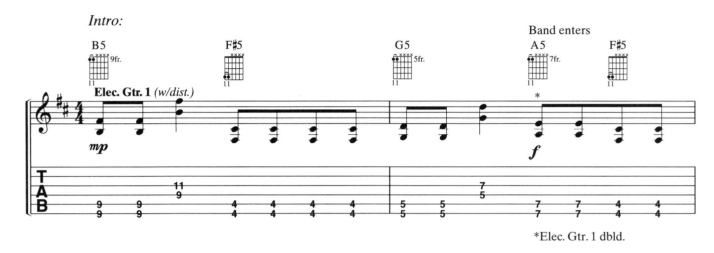

*Elec. Gtr. 1 dbld.

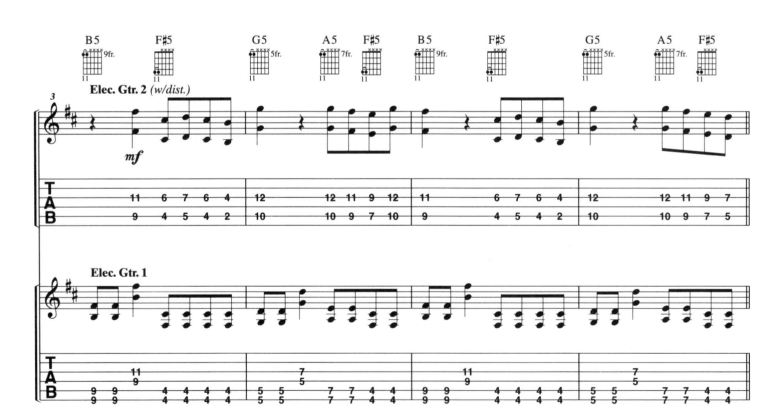

It's Not Me It's You - 9 - 1

Verse:

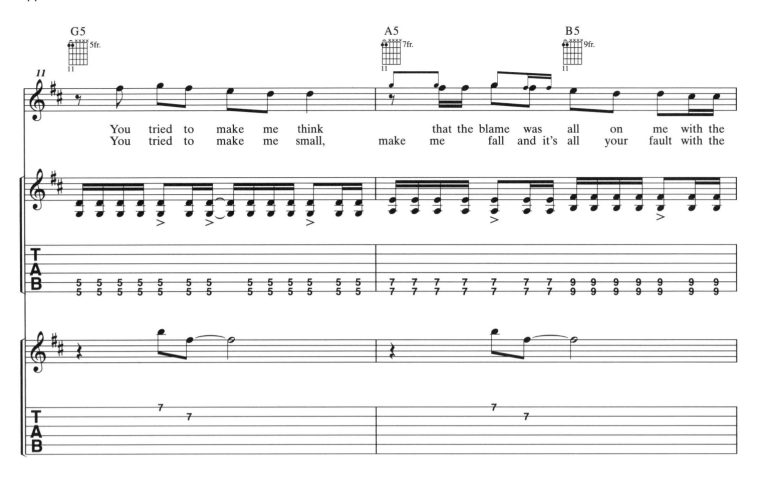

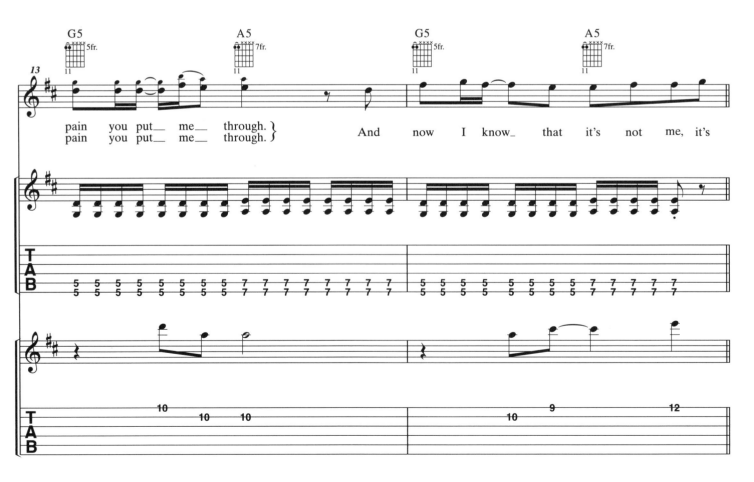

Chorus:

you. It's not me, it's you. Al - ways has been you. All the lies___ and

stu - pid things you say and do, it's you. It's not me, it's you. All the lies___ and

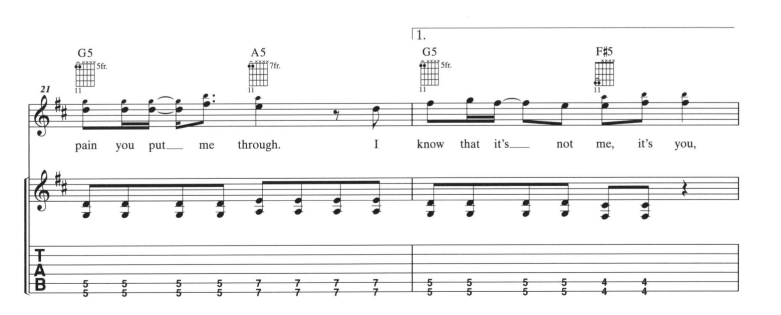

pain you put___ me through. I know that it's___ not me, it's you,

It's Not Me It's You - 9 - 4

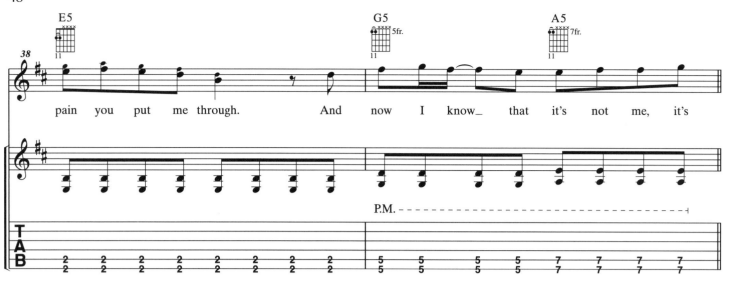

Chorus:

SHOULD'VE WHEN YOU COULD'VE

Chorus:

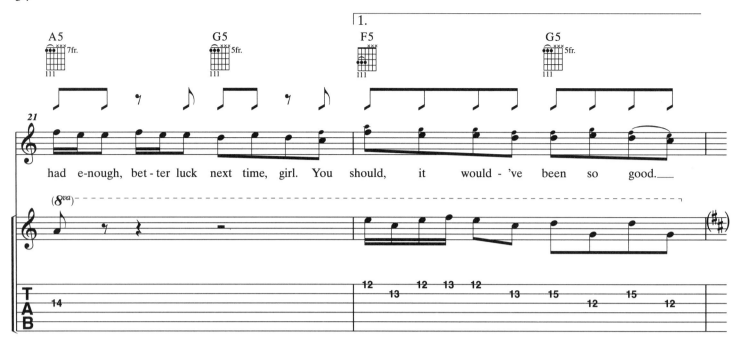

had e-nough, bet-ter luck next time, girl. You should, it would-'ve been so good.___

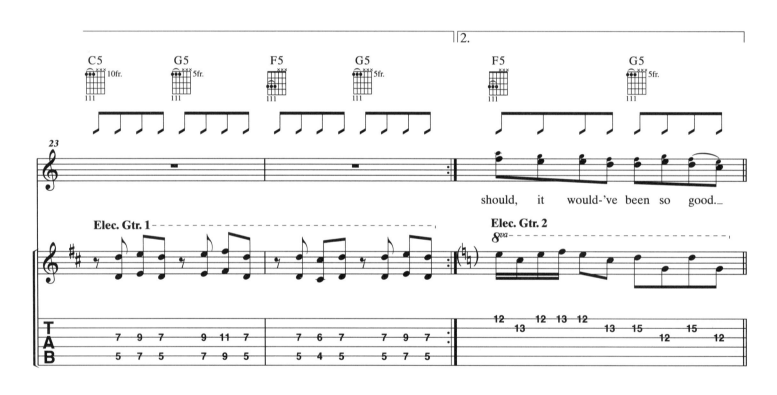

should, it would-'ve been so good._

Bridge:

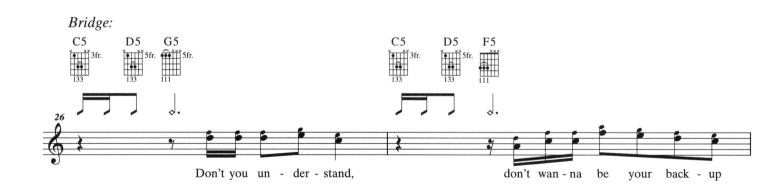

Don't you un-der-stand, don't wan-na be your back-up

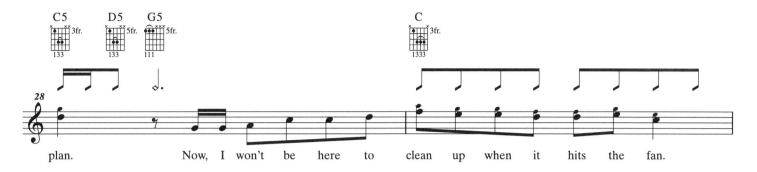

plan.   Now, I won't be here to clean up when it hits the fan.

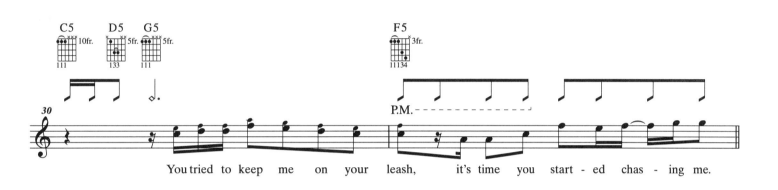

You tried to keep me on your leash, it's time you start - ed chas - ing me.

Instrumental:

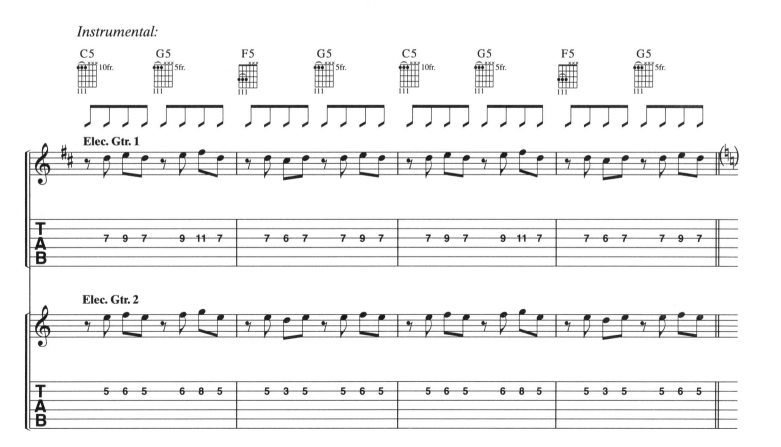

Verse 3:

Band tacet -

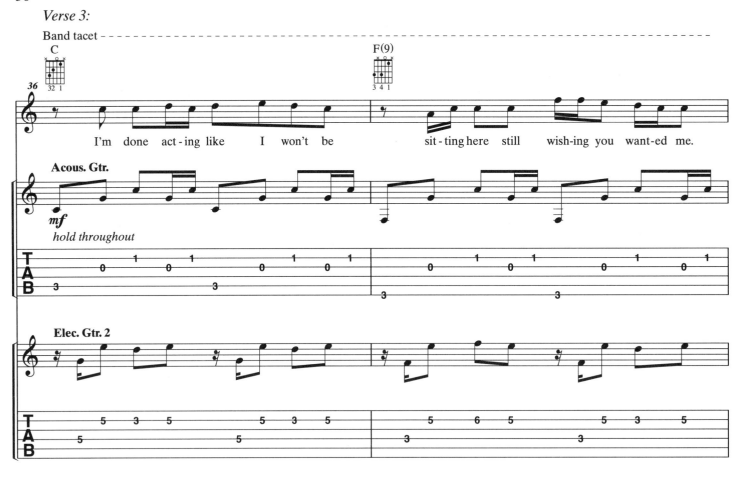

I'm done act-ing like I won't be sit-ting here still wish-ing you want-ed me.

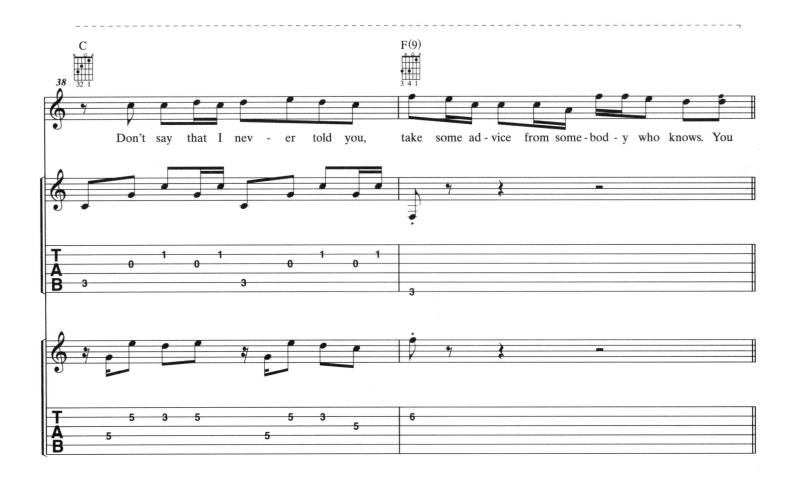

Don't say that I nev - er told you, take some ad-vice from some-bod-y who knows. You

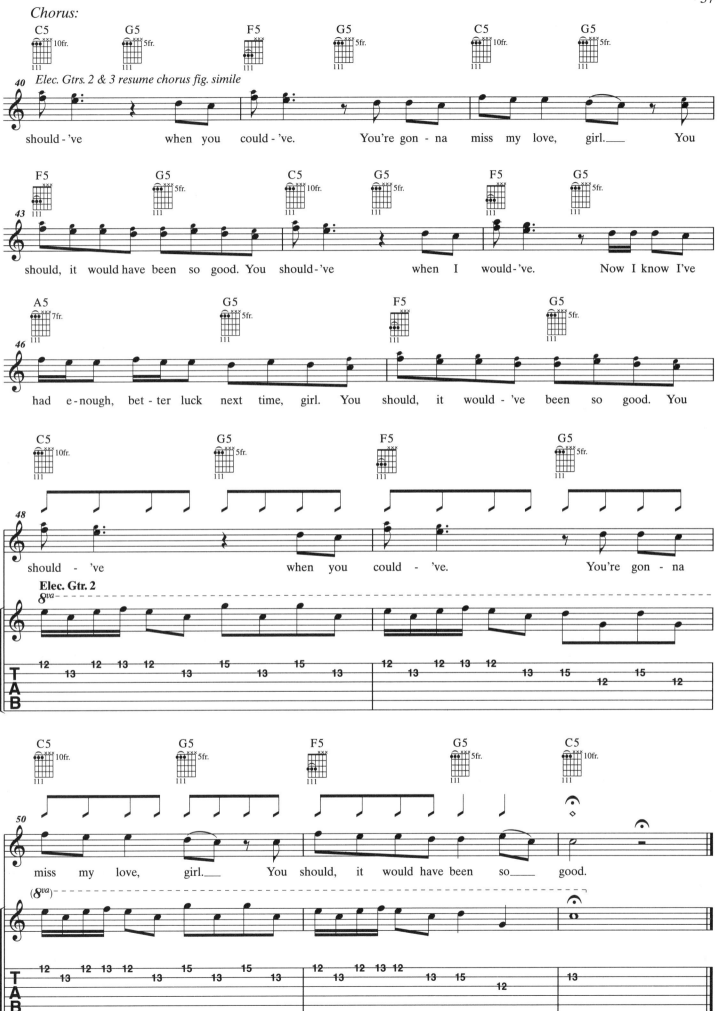

Chorus:

BELIEVE

All gtrs. in Drop D: ⑥ = D

Slow ♩ = 72

Intro:

Words and Music by
JOHN COOPER and DAVE BASSETT

Verses 1 & 2:

1. I'm still try-ing to fig-ure out____ how to tell you I____ was wrong.
2. I can't un-do the things____ that____ led us to____ this place.____

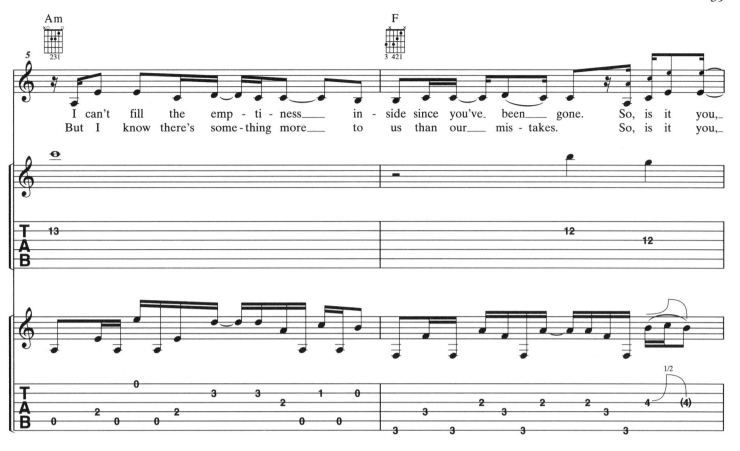

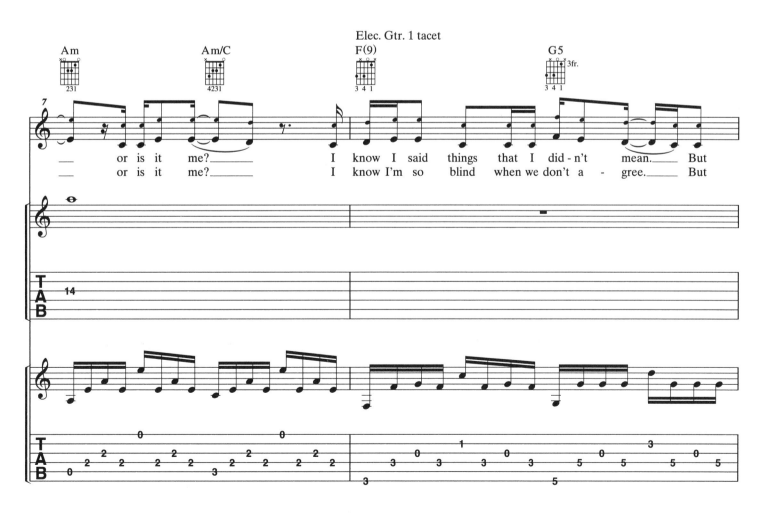

tell me that you___ still be - lieve.

Interlude:

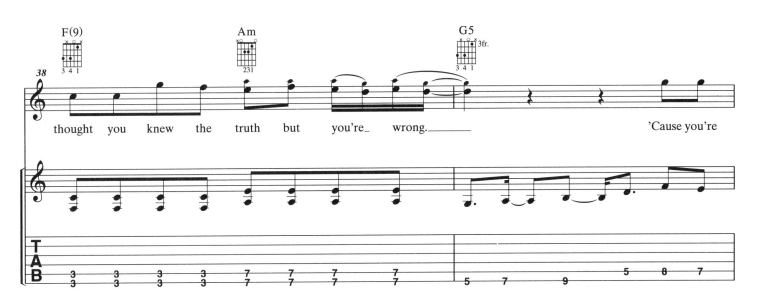

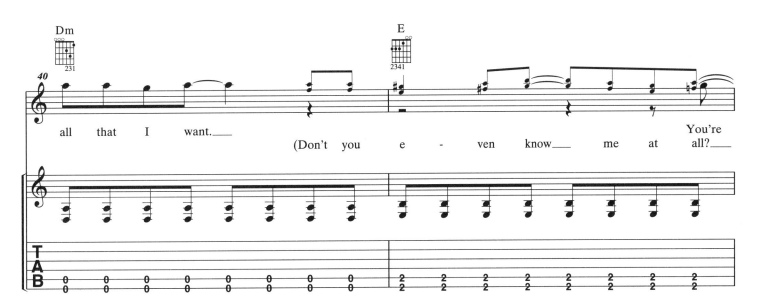

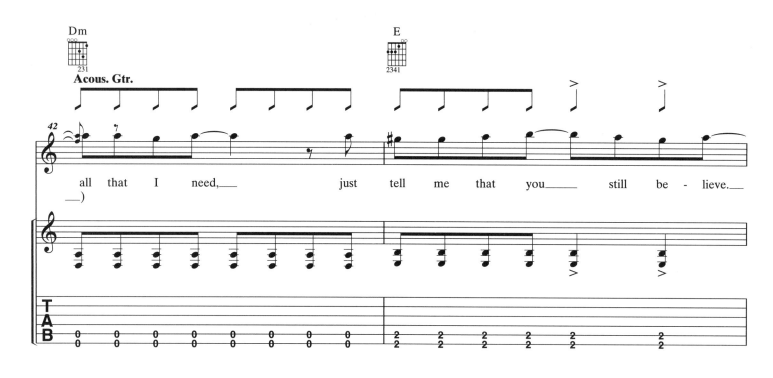

all that I need,___ just tell me that you___ still be - lieve.___
___)

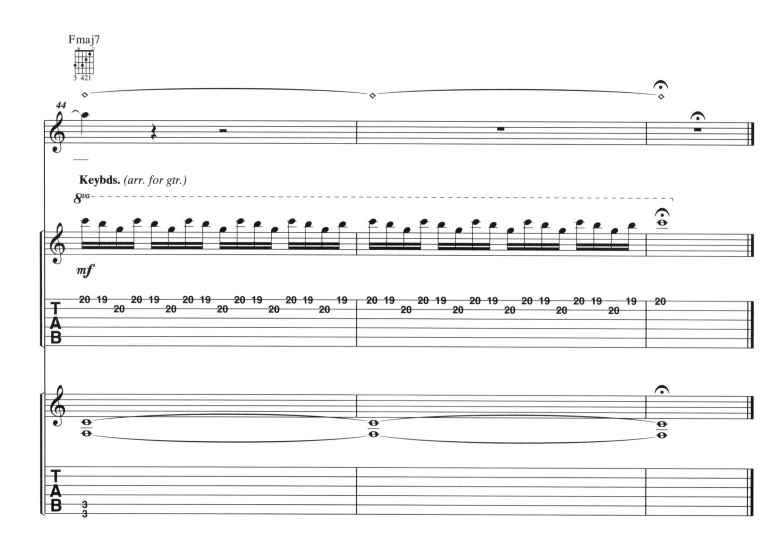

FORGIVEN

Words and Music by
JOHN COOPER

68

Forgiven - 7 - 2

Chorus:

Oh,__ whoa,__ whoa.__ Oh, oh,__ whoa,__ whoa.__ Oh,__ whoa,__ whoa.__ You have__ for-giv - en. For -

Outro: *Repeat and fade*

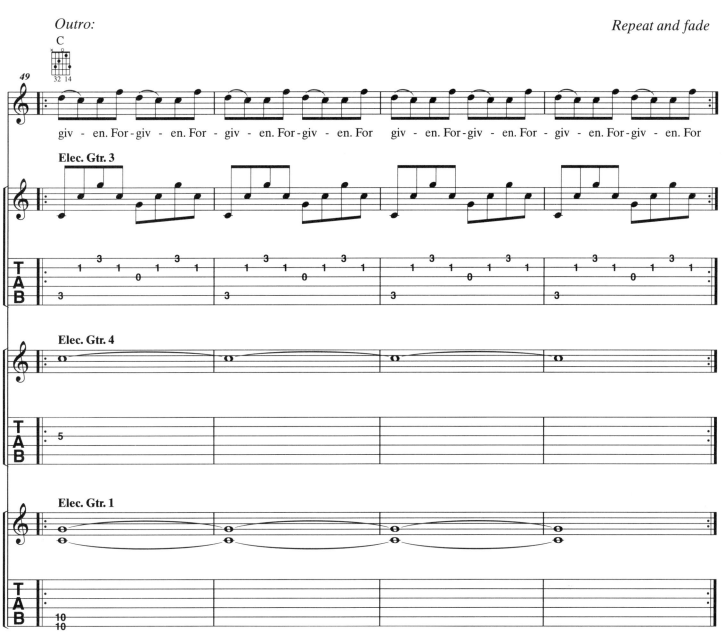

giv - en. For-giv - en. For - giv - en. For-giv - en. For giv - en. For-giv - en. For - giv - en. For-giv - en. For

Elec. Gtr. 3

Elec. Gtr. 4

Elec. Gtr. 1

SOMETIMES

*All gtrs. in Drop D, down 1 1/2 steps:

⑥ = B ③ = E
⑤ = F# ② = G#
④ = B ① = C#

Words and Music by
JOHN COOPER

Moderately slow ♩ = 84

Intro:

Recording sounds one and one half steps lower than written.

Chorus:

NEVER SURRENDER

All gtrs. in Drop D, down 1/2 step:

⑥ = D♭ ③ = G♭
⑤ = A♭ ② = B♭
④ = D♭ ① = E♭

Words and Music by
JOHN COOPER and DAVE BASSETT

Moderately slow ♩ = 84

Intro:

*Recording sounds a half step lower than written.

**Chords are implied.

*Cue-sized harmony notes 2nd time only.

Chorus:

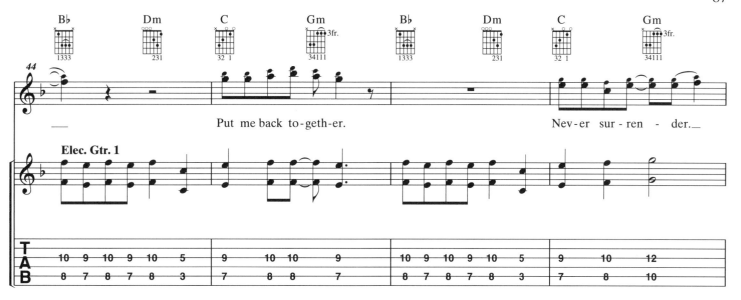

Put me back to-geth-er.   Nev-er sur-ren-der.__

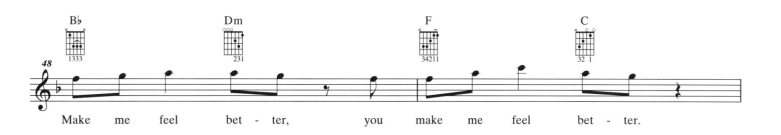

Make me feel bet - ter,   you make me feel bet - ter.

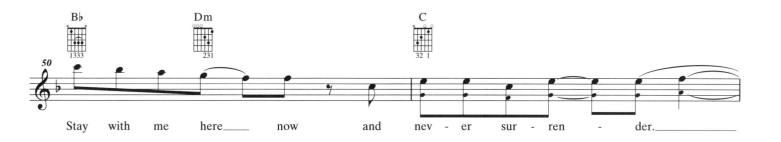

Stay with me here___ now   and nev - er sur - ren - der._____

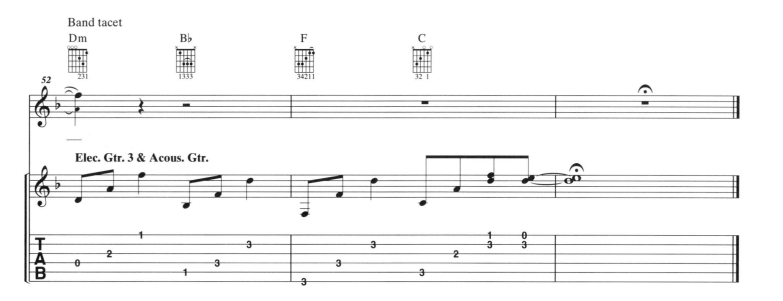

LUCY

Elec. Gtr. 2 in Drop D:
⑥ = D

Words and Music by
JOHN COOPER

Moderately slow ♩ = 76

Verse:

1. Hey, Lu-cy, I re-mem-ber your___ name.
2. Hey, Lu-cy, I re-mem-bered your birth-day.

I left a doz-en ros - es on your grave to-day.___
They said it brings some clo - sure to say your name.___

I'm in the grass on my knees, wipe the leaves a - way.___
I know I'd do it all dif-f'rent if I had the chance.___

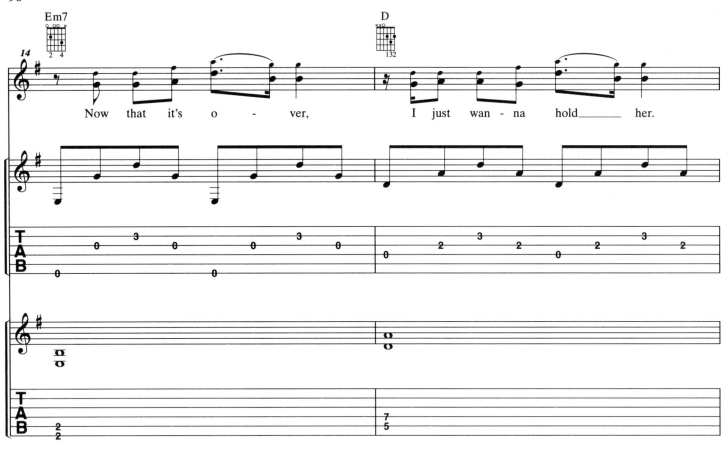

Now that it's o - ver, I just wan - na hold_____ her.

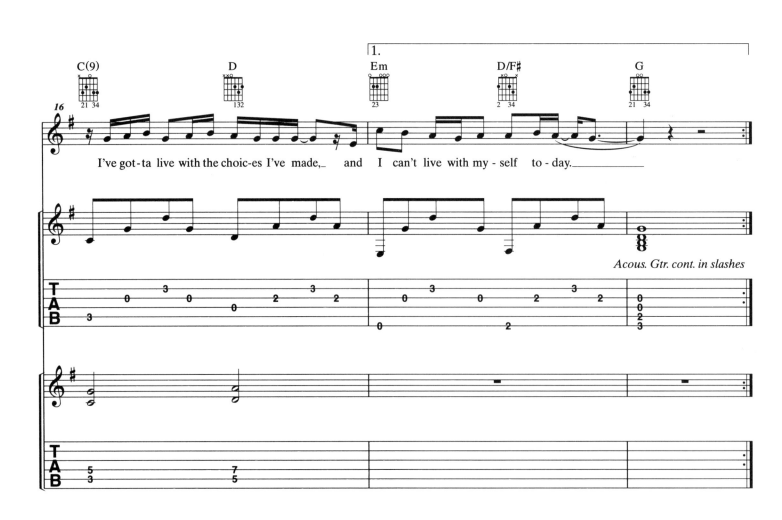

I've got-ta live with the choic-es I've made,_ and I can't live with my - self to - day._____

Acous. Gtr. cont. in slashes

Chorus:

Elec. Gtrs. 1 & 2, & Acous. Gtr. resume chorus fig. simile

Elec. Gtrs. 1 & 2, & Acous. Gtr.

Elec. Gtrs. 1 & 2, & Acous. Gtr. resume rhy. fig. simile

see you in an-oth-er life in heav-en_____ where we nev - er say_____ good -

bye. Now that it's o - ver, I just wan - na hold_____ her.

I'd give up all the world to see___ that lit - tle piece of heav-en look-ing back at me.

Now that it's o - ver, I just wan - na hold_____ her.

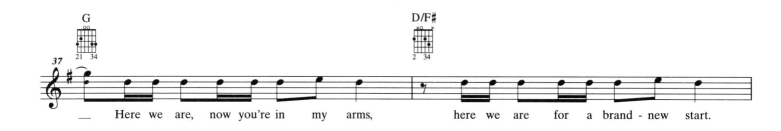

I've got - ta live with the choic - es I've made,_ and I can't live with my - self to - day._

_ Here we are, now you're in my arms, here we are for a brand - new start.

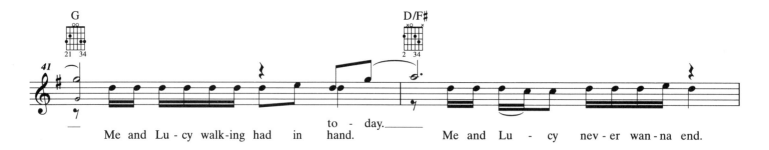

I've got - ta live with the choic - es I've made,_ and I can't live with my - self to - day,_

_ Me and Lu - cy walk - ing had in hand. to - day._ Me and Lu - cy nev - er wan - na end.

I've got - ta live with the choic - es I've made,_ and I can't live with my -

self to - day._ Hey, Lu - cy, I'll re - mem - ber your_ name.

TABLATURE EXPLANATION
TAB illustrates the six strings of the guitar.
Notes and chords are indicated by the placement of fret numbers on each string.

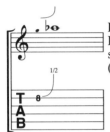

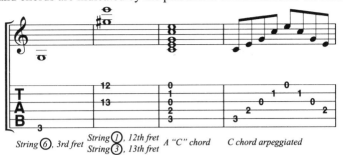

String ⑥, 3rd fret   *String ①, 12th fret*   *A "C" chord*   *C chord arpeggiated*
                       String ③, 13th fret

BENDING NOTES

Half Step:
Play the note and bend string one half step (one fret).

Whole Step:
Play the note and bend string one whole step (two frets).

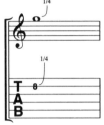

Slight Bend/ Quarter-Tone Bend:
Play the note and bend string sharp.

Prebend (Ghost Bend):
Bend to the specified note before the string is plucked.

Prebend and Release:
Play the already-bent string, then immediately drop it down to the fretted note.

Unison Bends:
Play both notes and immediately bend the lower note to the same pitch as the higher note.

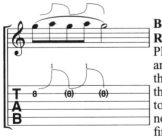

Bend and Release:
Play the note and bend to the next pitch, then release to the original note. Only the first note is attacked.

Bends Involving More Than One String:
Play the note and bend the string while playing an additional note on another string. Upon release, relieve the pressure from the additional note allowing the original note to sound alone.

Bends Involving Stationary Notes:
Play both notes and immediately bend the lower note up to pitch. Return as indicated.

ARTICULATIONS

Hammer On:
Play the lower note, then "hammer" your finger to the higher note. Only the first note is plucked.

Pull Off:
Play the higher note with your first finger already in position on the lower note. Pull your finger off the first note with a strong downward motion that plucks the string—sounding the lower note.

Legato Slide:
Play the first note and, keeping pressure applied on the string, slide up to the second note. The diagonal line shows that it is a slide and not a hammer-on or a pull-off.

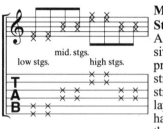

Muted Strings:
A percussive sound is produced by striking the strings while laying the fret hand across them.

Palm Mute:
The notes are muted (muffled) by placing the palm of the pick hand lightly on the strings, just in front of the bridge.

HARMONICS

Natural Harmonic:
A finger of the fret hand lightly touches the string at the note indicated in the TAB and is plucked by the pick producing a bell-like sound called a harmonic.

RHYTHM SLASHES

Strum Marks/ Rhythm Slashes:
Strum with the indicated rhythm pattern. Strum marks can be located above the staff or within the staff.

Single Notes with Rhythm Slashes:
Sometimes single notes are incorporated into a strum pattern. The circled number below is the string and the fret number is above.

Artificial Harmonic:
Fret the note at the first TAB number, lightly touch the string at the fret indicated in parens (usually 12 frets higher than the fretted note), then pluck the string with an available finger or your pick.

TREMOLO BAR

Specified Interval:
The pitch of a note or chord is lowered to the specified interval and then return as indicated. The action of the tremolo bar is graphically represented by the peaks and valleys of the diagram.

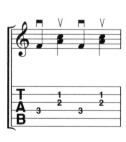

Unspecified Interval:
The pitch of a note or chord is lowered, usually very dramatically, until the pitch of the string becomes indeterminate.

PICK DIRECTION

Downstrokes and Upstrokes:
The downstroke is indicated with this symbol (⊓) and the upstroke is indicated with this (V).